Because Jesus Christ was
RESURRECTED
I will be too!

Joseph Smith Translated The Book of Mormon

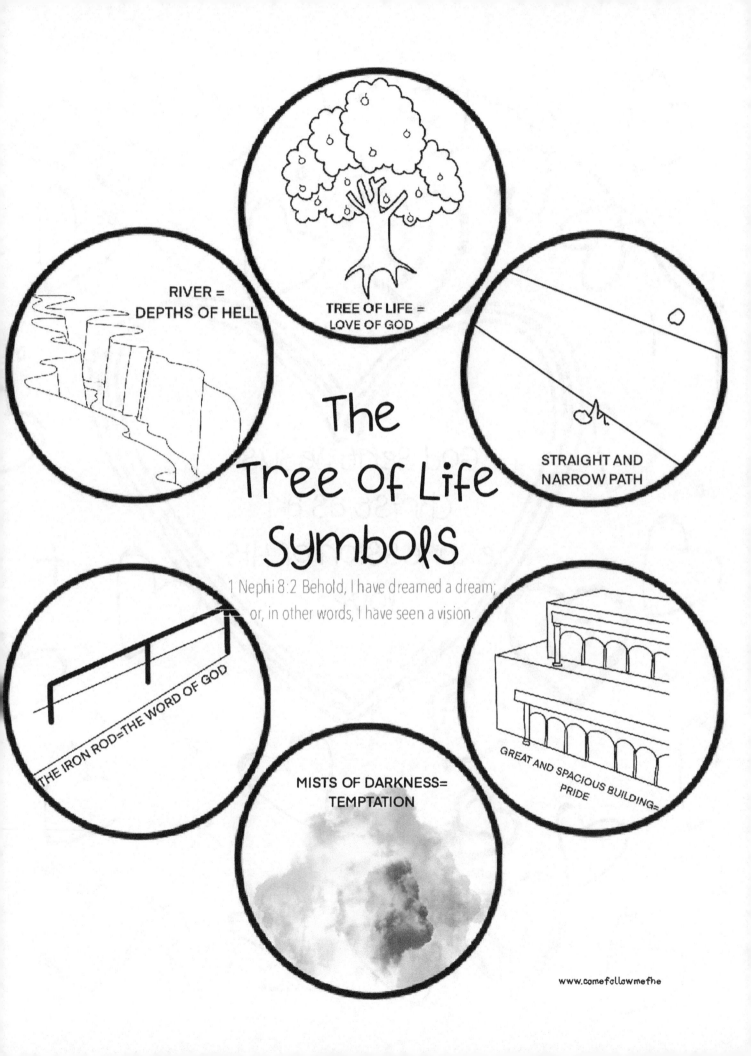

RIVER =
DEPTHS OF HELL

TREE OF LIFE =
LOVE OF GOD

STRAIGHT AND
NARROW PATH

The
Tree Of Life
Symbols

1 Nephi 8:2 Behold, I have dreamed a dream; or, in other words, I have seen a vision.

THE IRON ROD=THE WORD OF GOD

MISTS OF DARKNESS=
TEMPTATION

GREAT AND SPACIOUS BUILDING=
PRIDE

God Sent Jesus Christ as an expression of His love.

www.comefollowmefhe

2 Nephi 3:6-24

Joseph of Egypt prophesied of Joseph Smith.
2 Nephi 3: 14-15

14 And thus prophesied Joseph, saying: Behold, that seer will the Lord bless; and they that seek to destroy him shall be confounded; for this promise, which I have obtained of the Lord, of the fruit of my loins, shall be fulfilled. Behold, I am sure of the fulfilling of this promise; 15 And his name shall be called after me; and it shall be after the name of his father. And he shall be like unto me; for the thing, which the Lord shall bring forth by his hand, by the power of the Lord shall bring my people unto salvation.

What do these verses teach me about the importance of The Book of Mormon?

_____

_____

_____

_____

_____

_____

2 Nephi 25:26

AND WE TALK OF CHRIST,

WE REJOICE IN CHRIST,

WE PREACH OF CHRIST,

WE PROPHESY OF CHRIST,

AND WE WRITE ACCORDING TO OUR

PROPHECIES, THAT OUR CHILDREN

MAY KNOW TO WHAT SOURCE

THEY MAY LOOK

FOR A REMISSION OF THEIR SINS.

2 Nephi 9:9-10

Jesus Christ saves me from sin and death.
He bridges the gap for me to return to Heavenly Father.

www.comefollowmefhe

2 Nephi 27:6-7

6 And it shall come to pass that the Lord God shall bring forth unto you the words of a book, and they shall be the words of them which have slumbered.

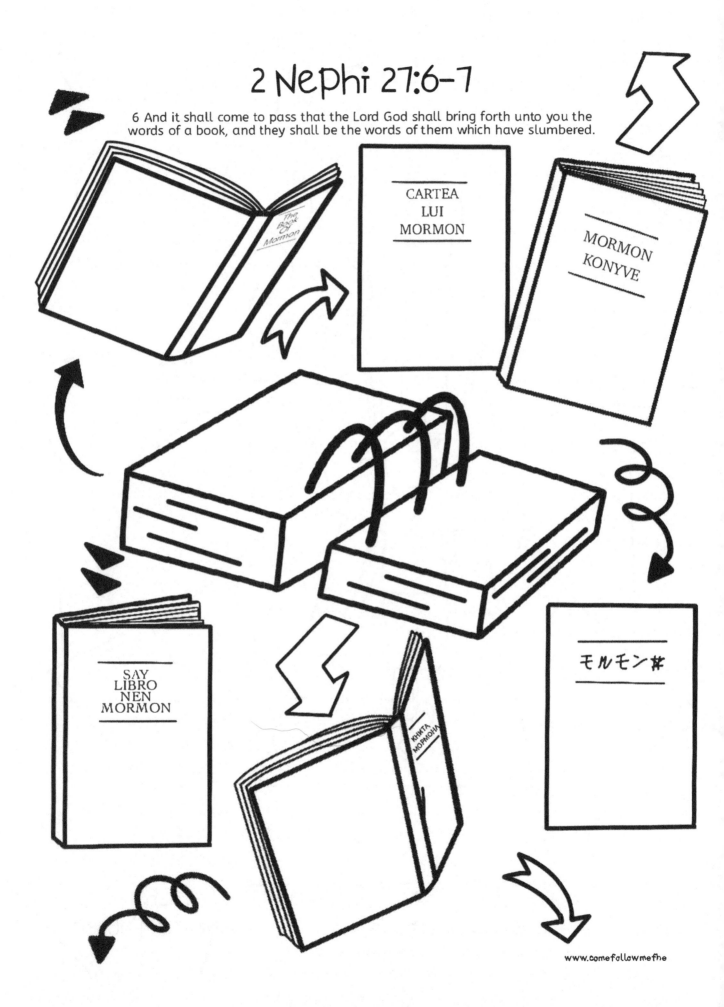

My Family Tree

DRAW YOUR OWN FAMILY TREE

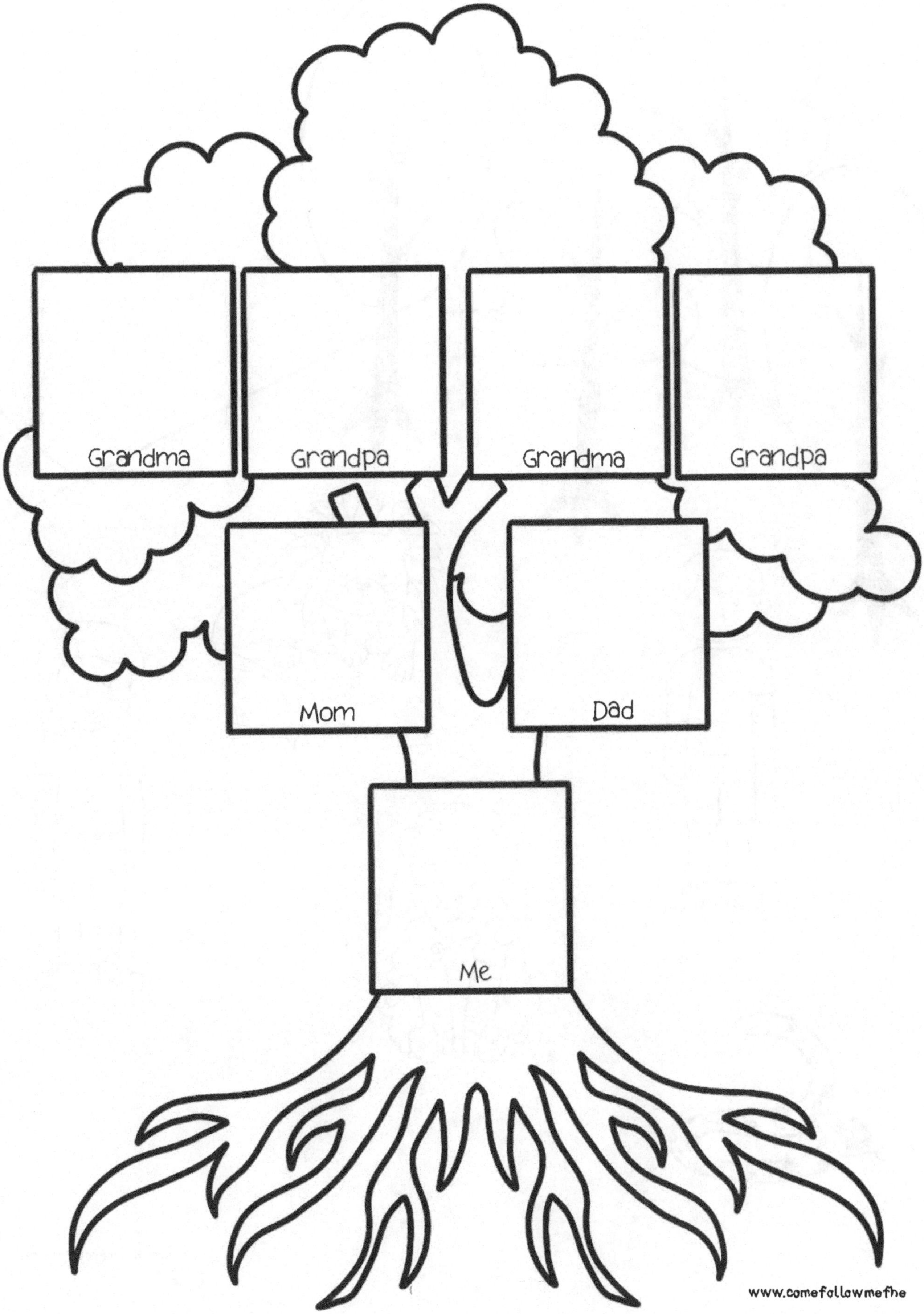

Grandma
Grandpa
Grandma
Grandpa
Mom
Dad
Me

www.comefollowmefhe

2 NEPHI 21:6-9

www.comefollowmefhe

2 Nephi 31:4-13

Jesus Christ set the perfect example of obedience when He was baptized

2 Nephi 31:4-13

Jesus Christ set the perfect example of obedience when He was baptized

www.comefollowmefhe

He is not here, for he is risen.

Matthew 28:6

BEE

a covenant keeper

Mosiah 8: 5-12

"Limhi's people found the 24 plates of gold from the Jaredites"

Mosiah 8: 5-12

"Limhi's people found the 24 plates of gold from the Jaredites"

The Lord provided us with a prophet seer and revelator THEN

And He does so NOW

Mosiah 8:12-19

I can follow Jesus Christ by standing for the right

I can prepare now to make and keep covenants

I can learn about covenants

I can go to primary

I can love like Jesus

I can read the Scriptures

I can pay my tithing

I can serve others

I can say my prayers

Draw yourself being baptized

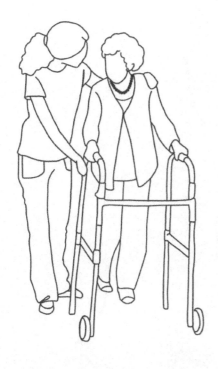

I can be a
missionary now!

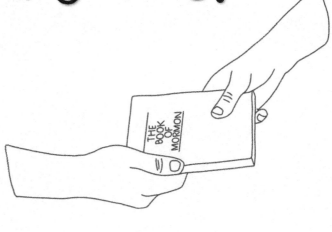

Alma 11:43-44

Alma 14:8–11

"Whosoever believed or had been taught to believe in the word of God, they caused that they should be cast into the fire."

The Lord will bless me when I keep the commandments

Alma 17: 9-10

KING LAMONI

AMMON

Aaron teaches basic gospel principles to Lamoni's father, the king

Alma 22:4-18

As you read Alma 20 aloud, draw or describe what is taking place along the path and in the Land of Middoni.

(Ex. Draw Ammon's imprisoned brethren behind bars)

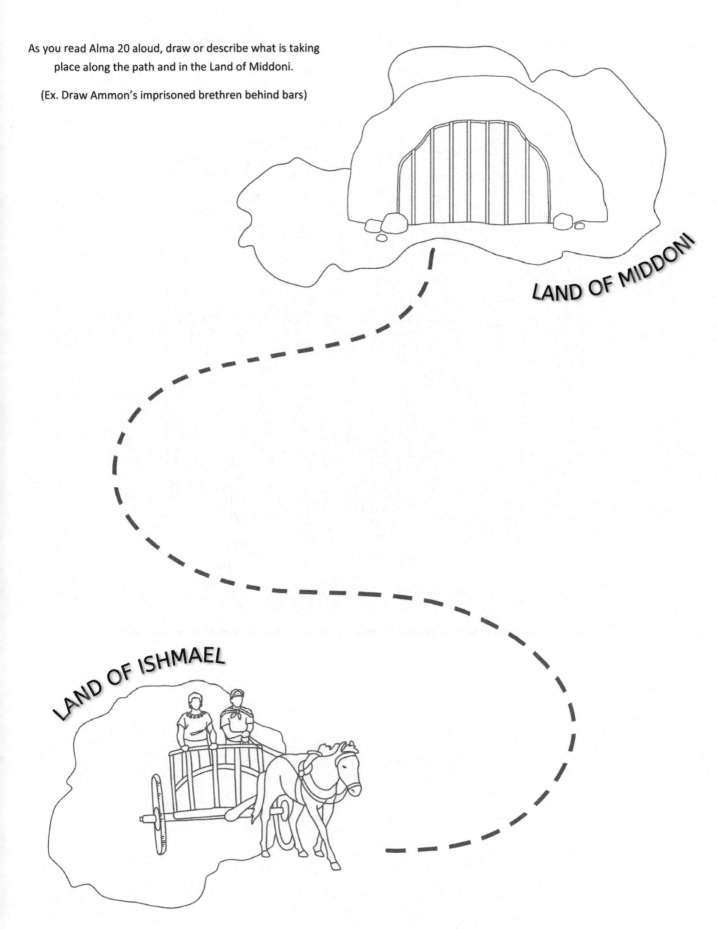

LAND OF MIDDONI

LAND OF ISHMAEL

The Anti-Nephi-Lehies buried their weapons to follow the Lord.
Alma 24:6-24

Draw the buried weapons below the ground.

Jesus Christ came to earth to be my Savior

www.comefollowmefhe.com

All Things Testify of God

All Things Testify of God

Because Jesus was Resurrected, I Will Be Too.

Alma 40:23

www.comefollowmefhe.com

The Scriptures teach me How to PRAY

Alma 30-31

Heavenly Father Hears
and Answers My prayers

Heavenly Father Hears and Answers my prayers

Meal

Bedtime

Church

School

Repentance brings me joy!

Alma 36:6, 20, 24

Repentance brings me joy!

Alma 36:6, 20, 24

I can be Faithful to God Like the Stripling Warriors.

Alma 53: 20-21

Help my mother.

Spend time with loved ones.

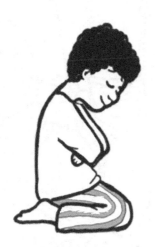

The Lord wants me to remember Him.

Be a good friend.

Pray daily.

Serve others.

Help in my community.

prophets teach about
Jesus Christ

Moses

Abinadi

Joseph Smith

The prophets' words are always fulfilled. 3 Nephi 1:20

Daniel

Noah

Nephi

Destructions in the Land Matching

"And many great destructions have I caused to come upon this land, and upon this people, because of their wickedness and abominations" (3 Nephi 9:12)

Read 3 Nephi 9:1-12 and draw a line from the cities on the left to the matching destruction on the right.

CITIES OF:

MORONIHAH, GILGAL, GADIANDI, GADIOMNAH, JACOB, AND GIMGIMNO

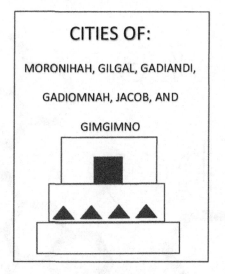

CITIES OF:

MORONI, ONIHAH, MOCUM AND JERUSALEM

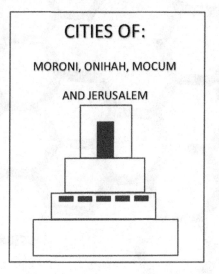

CITIES OF:

ZARAHEMLA, JACOBUGATH, LAMAN JOSH, GAD AND KISHKUMEN

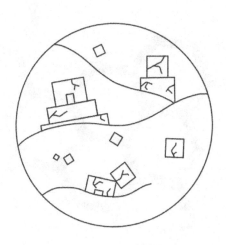

Blessed Are They

The Savior loves all children

3 Nephi 17:11-12

My Heavenly Father Wants me to Learn About My Ancestors

Ask my grandparents about their history.

Write down my own history.

Use Family Search to find my ancestors.

Go to the temple and perform work for the dead.

Ways to learn about my ancestors

Read my family history.

www.comefollowmefhe.com

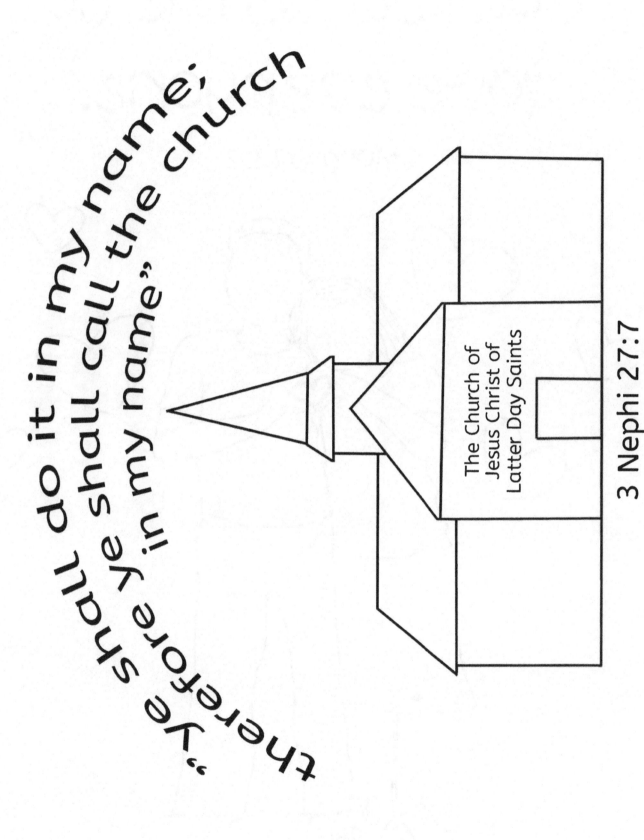

"Ye shall do it in my name; therefore ye shall call the church in my name;"

The Church of Jesus Christ of Latter Day Saints

3 Nephi 27:7

God wants me to love everyone.

Mormon 3:12

GUIDE TO HAPPINESS

BEING HONEST

HAVING THE HOLY GHOST

LOVE OF GOD

NO CONTENTION

GOING TO CHURCH

FASTING AND PRAYING

KEEPING COMMANDMENTS

"And surely there could not be a happier people among all the people who had been created by the hand of God"
(4 Nephi 1:16)

N E S W

I Belong to the Church of Jesus Christ of Latter-Day Saints

Name _____

Date of Birth _____

Primary Teacher _____

MY FAVORITE

Part about being a member

_____

_____

Primary Song _____

_____

Scripture _____

Article of Faith _____

Temple _____

What do you love about the
Come Follow Me Study at home?

_____

_____

_____

I Belong to the Church of Jesus Christ of Latter-Day Saints

Name _____

Date of Birth _____

Primary Teacher _____

MY FAVORITE

Part about being a member

_____

_____

Primary Song _____

_____

Scripture _____

Article of Faith _____

Temple _____

What do you love about the
Come Follow Me Study at home?

_____

_____

_____

Draw yourself in Christ's arms.

I can choose the right even when I feel alone!

"I AM CREATED IN GOD'S IMAGE"

– ETHER 3

Follow the instructions below on both figures above:

[ ] Draw a circle around the feet
[ ] Color in the hair
[ ] Draw a square around the hands

[ ] Draw an arrow pointing at the eyes
[ ] Draw a heart on the chest
[ ] Color in the body

"I AM CREATED IN GOD'S IMAGE"

– ETHER 3

Follow the instructions below on both figures above:

[ ] Draw a circle around the feet
[ ] Color in the hair
[ ] Draw a square around the hands

[ ] Draw an arrow pointing at the eyes
[ ] Draw a heart on the chest
[ ] Color in the body

Heavenly Father

COMFORTS

me

when i am

SCARED

and

SMALL

Ether 6:2-12

Ether 12:7

Ether 12:11

Ether 12:20-21

Faith
is things
which are
hoped for and
not seen.
Ether 12:6

Ether 12:13

Ether 12:8-9

Ether 12:14

www.comefollowmefhe.com

THE HOLY GHOST IS A SACRED GIFT

I can have hope in Christ regardless of my circumstances!

Moroni 9:25-26

Help Moroni bury the plates.

Cut along the dotted lines, and the strip below. Feed the strip through from the back over this text from right to left to help Moroni bury the golden plates.

OLIVE TREE ALLEGORY
JACOB 5

Eternal marriage

Prayer

Love of God

Repentance

I CAN GAIN A TESTIMONY OF MY OWN

The Holy Ghost

Baptism

www.comefollowmefhe

Made in the USA
Las Vegas, NV
01 March 2024

86342092R00039